SAGUARO NATIONAL PARK
ACTIVITY BOOK

PUZZLES, MAZES, GAMES, AND MORE ABOUT SAGUARO NATIONAL PARK

NATIONAL PARKS ACTIVITIES SERIES

SAGUARO NATIONAL PARK

ACTIVITY BOOK

Copyright 2022
Published by Little Bison Press

The author acknowledges that the land on which Saguaro National Park is located are the traditional lands of Tohono O'odham, Sobaipuri, O'odham Jeweḍ, and Hohokam Tribes.

LITTLE BISON
Press

For more free national parks activities, visit
Littlebisonpress.com

About Saguaro National Park

Saguaro National Park (pronounced suh-waa-row) is located in the heart of the Sonoran desert, in the state of Arizona. The park's namesake is the largest cactus in the world, the giant saguaro.

This park is famous for being home to over 2 million saguaro cacti. They are native only to the Sonoran desert. Usually, they can grow up to 40 feet tall but the tallest one ever recorded was 78 feet tall. The average age of a saguaro cactus is between 150 and 175 years old! The park is also home to hundreds of diverse plants and animals. It is a popular place to hike and camp year-round.

The park consists of two separate parcels, sandwiched on either side of the city of Tucson, Arizona. The Tucson Mountain District (TMD) is called Saguaro West and contains the famous saguaro forest. The Rincon Mountain District (RMD) is known as Saguaro East and is more remote and mountainous than Saguaro West. Combined, they cover over 90,000 acres of a desert landscape.

Saguaro National Park is famous for:
- giant saguaro cactus
- tall mountain peaks
- beautiful desert landscapes

Hey! I'm Parker!

I'm the only snail in history to visit every National Park in the United States! Come join me on my adventures in Saguaro National Park.

Throughout this book, we will learn about the history of the park, the animals and plants that live here, and things to do here if you ever get to visit in person. This book is also full of games and activities!

Last but not least, I am hidden 9 times on different pages. See how many times you can find me. This page doesn't count!

Saguaro Bingo

Let's play bingo! Cross off each box that you are able to during your visit to the national park. Try to get a bingo down, across, or diagonally. If you can't visit the park, use the bingo board to plan your perfect trip.

Pick out some activities that you would want to do during your visit. What would you do first? How long would you spend there? What animals would you try to see?

SPOT A DESERT TORTISE	SEE A GIANT SAGUARO	IDENTIFY A TREE	TAKE A PICTURE AT AN OVERLOOK	WATCH A MOVIE AT THE VISITORS CENTER
GO FOR A HIKE	LEARN ABOUT THE INDIGENOUS PEOPLE THAT LIVE IN THIS AREA	WITNESS A SUNRISE OR SUNSET	OBSERVE THE NIGHT SKIES	GO BIRD WATCHING
HEAR A BIRD CALL	SPOT A TALL MOUNTAIN	FREE SPACE	LEARN ABOUT THE IMPORTANCE OF THE SAGUARO	SPOT SOME ANIMAL TRACKS
PICK UP TEN PIECES OF TRASH	HAVE A PICNIC	SEE A JAVELINA	HIKE TO A LIME KILN	SPOT A BIRD OF PREY
LEARN ABOUT THE GEOLOGY OF THE DESERT	SEE SOMEONE RIDING A HORSE	GO CAMPING	VISIT A RANGER STATION	PARTICIPATE IN A RANGER-LED ACTIVITY

The National Park Logo

The National Park System has over 400 units in the US. Just like Saguaro National Park, each location is unique or special in some way. The areas include other national parks, historic sites, monuments, seashores, and other recreation areas.

Each element of the National Park emblem represents something that the National Park Service protects. Fill in each blank below to show what each symbol represents.

```
WORD BANK:

MOUNTAINS, ARROWHEAD, BISON,
SEQUOIA TREE, WATER
```

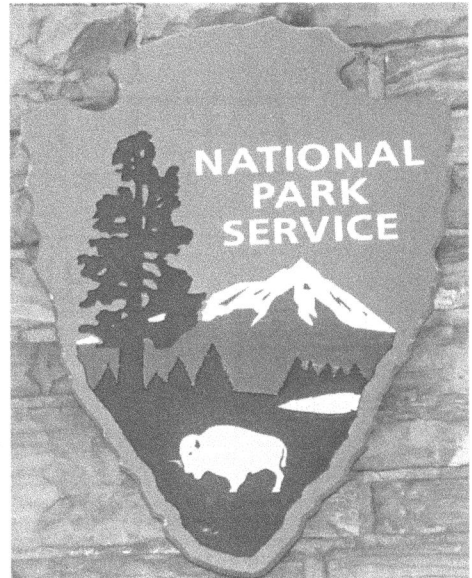

This represents all plants. _____

This represents all animals. _____

This symbol represents the landscapes. _____

This represents the waters protected by the park service. _____

This represents the historical and archeological values. _____

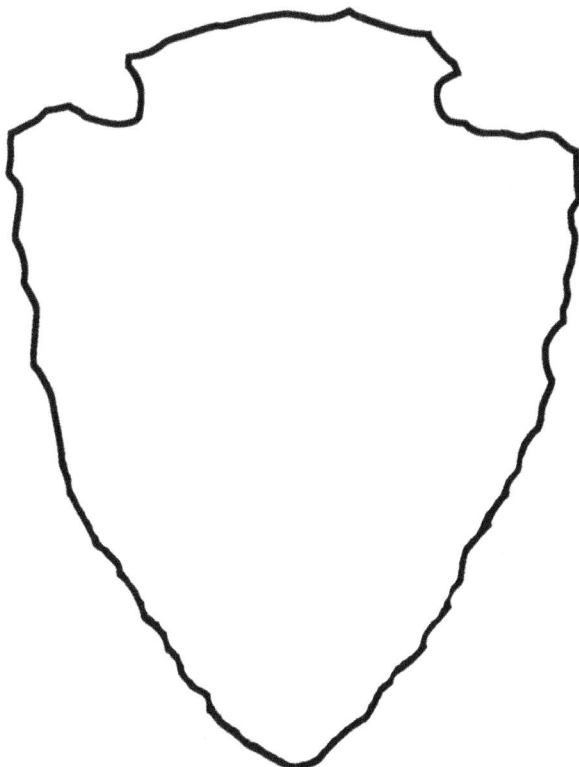

Now it's your turn! Pretend you are designing a new national park. Add elements to the design that represent the things that your park protects

What is the name of your park?

Describe why you included the symbols that you included. What do they mean?

Things to Do Jumble

Unscramble the letters to uncover activities you can do while in Saguaro National Park. Hint: each one ends in -ing.

1. DRAE
   ☐☐☐☐ ING

2. KHI
   ☐☐☐ ING

3. RIBD
   ☐☐☐☐ ING

4. PAMC
   ☐☐☐☐ ING

5. CCIPNKI
   ☐☐☐☐☐☐☐ ING

6. SSGHITEE
   ☐☐☐☐☐☐☐☐ ING

7. SARTGZA
   ☐☐☐☐☐☐☐ ING

Word Bank

birding

reading

camping

stargazing

horseback riding

hiking

hunting

singing

yelling

sightseeing

picnicking

Color the Saguaros

Did you know the saguaro cactus produces fruit? Birds, bats, and other mammals eat this sweet fruit. People from the Tohono O'odham Tribe have harvested saguaro fruit in the Sonoran Desert for thousands of years, long before Saguaro National Park was established.

Go Birdwatching at Bridal Wreath Falls

start here

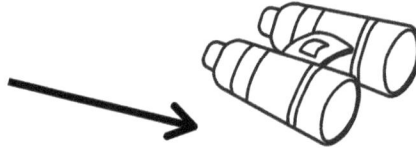

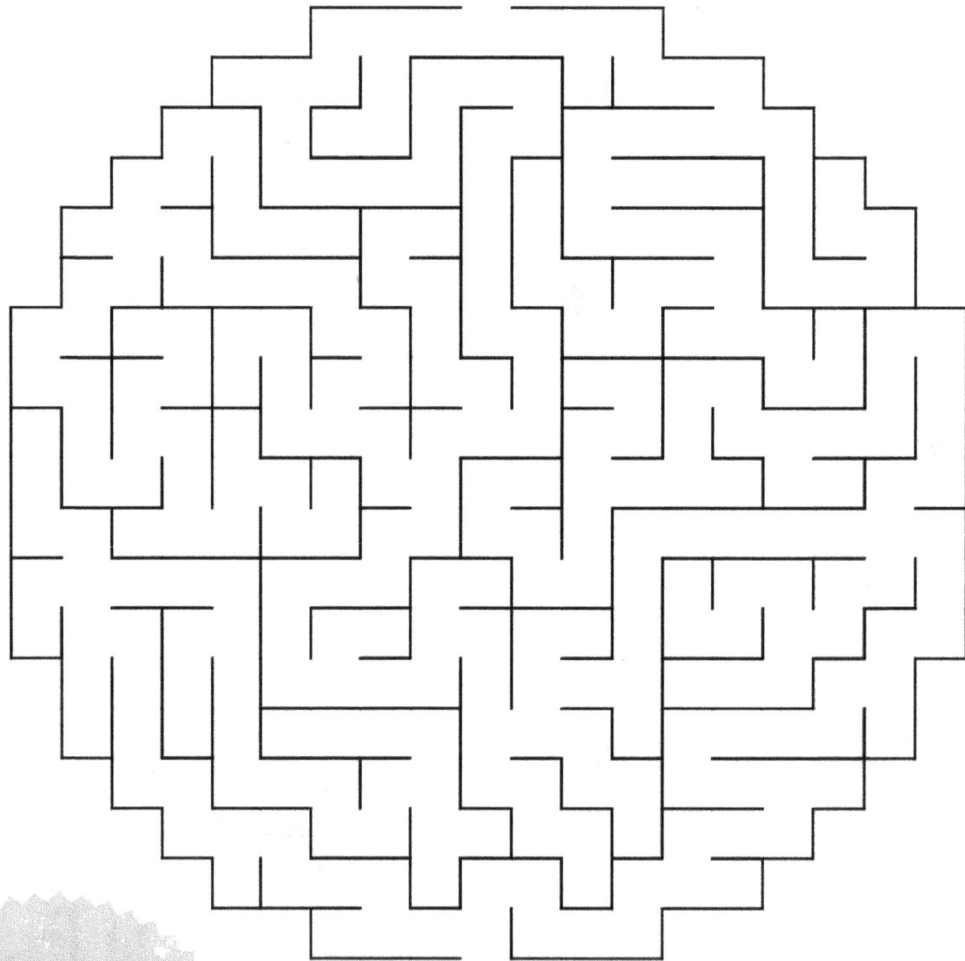

DID YOU KNOW?
Saguaro National Park is home to several birds of prey, including eagles, hawks, and owls. Birds of prey are birds that hunt other animals for food.

Camping Packing List

What should you take with you camping? Pretend you are in charge of your family camping trip. Make a list of what you would need to be safe and comfortable on an overnight excursion. Some considerations are listed on the side.

1.
2.
3.
4.
5.
6.
7.
8.
9.
10.
11.
12.
13.
14.
15.
16.

- What will you eat at every meal?

- What will the weather be like?

- Where will you sleep?

- What will you do during your free time?

- How luxurious do you want camp to be?

- How will you cook?

- How will you see at night?

- How will you dispose of trash?

- What might you need in case of emergencies?

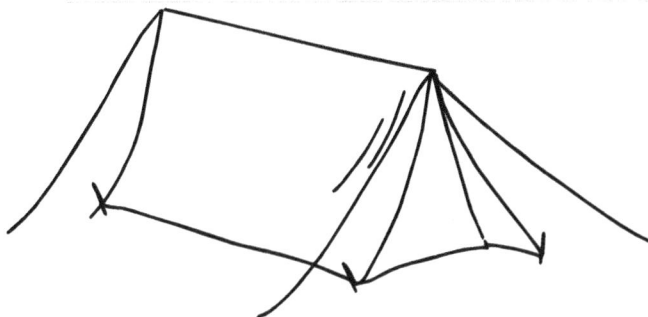

Camping at Saguaro NP is not for the faint of heart! It requires a backcountry permit and you will need to hike into your campsite.

Saguaro National Park

Date: _____   Season: _____

Who I went with: _____   Which entrance: _____

How was your experience? Write a few sentences on your trip. Where did you stay? What did you do? What was your favorite activity? If you have not yet visited the park, write a paragraph pretending that you did.

_____

_____

_____

_____

_____

STAMPS

Many national parks and monuments have cancellation stamps for visitors to use. These rubber stamps record the date and the location that you visited. Many people collect the markings as a free souvenir. Check with a ranger to see where you can find a stamp during your visit. If you aren't able to find one, you can draw your own.

Where is the Park?

Saguaro National Park is in the southwest United States. It is located in the landlocked desert state of Arizona.

Arizona

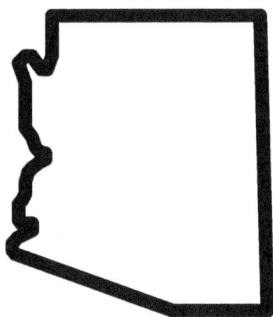

Look at the shape of Arizona. Can you find it on the map? If you are from the US, can you find your home state? Color Arizona red. Color every state that borders Arizona orange. Put a star on the map where you live. Color the rest of the states any way you'd like.

Connect the Dots #1

Connect the dots to figure out what this tiny critter is. There are eight types of these that live in Saguaro National Park.

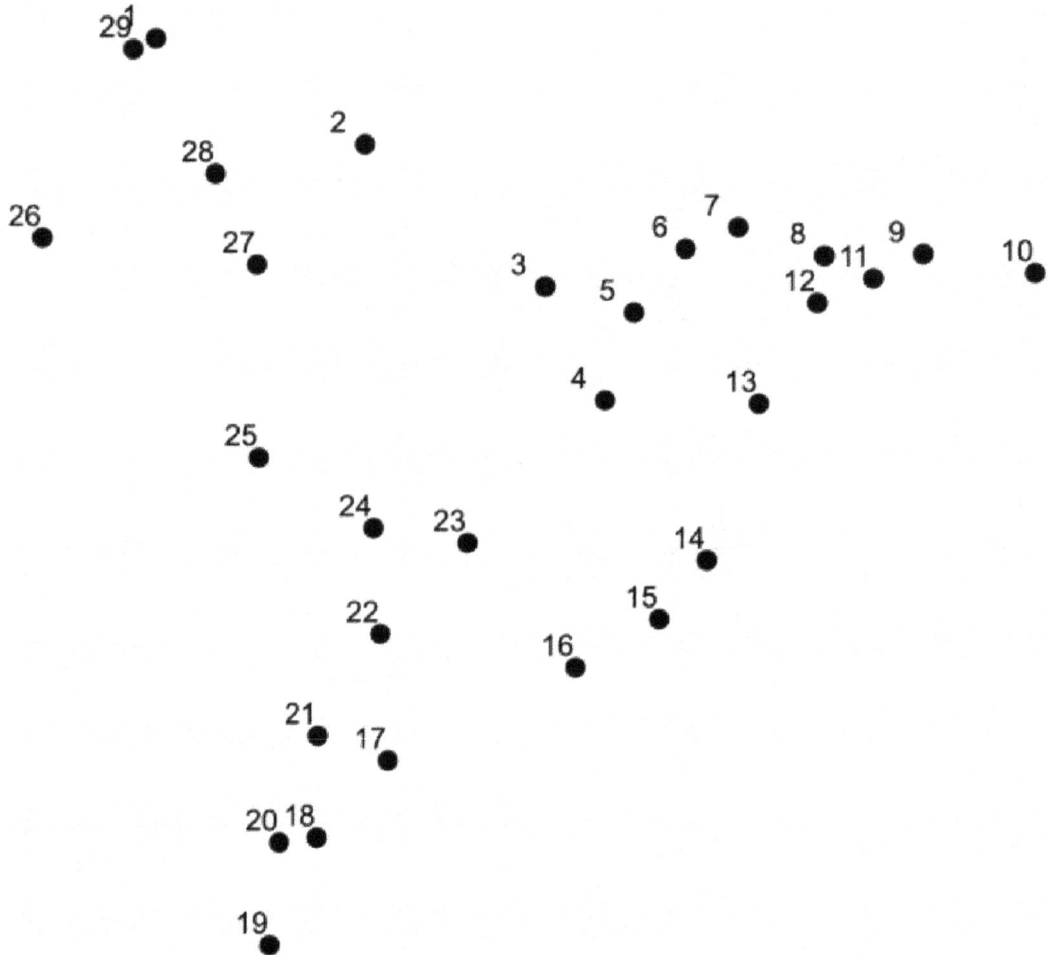

29 1
2
28
26
27
6 7 8 9 10
3 11
5 12
4 13
25
24 23 14
15
22 16
21 17
20 18
19

Their heart rate can reach as high as 1,260 beats per minute and a breathing rate of 250 breaths per minute. Have you ever measured your breathing rate? Ask a friend or family member to set a timer for 60 seconds. Once they say "go", try to breathe normally. Count each breath until they say "stop." How do your breaths per minute compare to hummingbirds?

_____

_____

The coati is a relative of the raccoon. They feed by using their long noses, poking them under rocks and into crevices.

Hummingbirds are the smallest migrating birds. The average weight of a hummingbird is less than a nickel!

Who lives here?

Here are seven plants and animals that live in the park.
Use the word bank to fill in the clues below.

WORD BANK: HUMMINGBIRD, COATI, SCORPION, GILA MONSTER
BOBCAT, GRAY FOX, SAGUARO

▢▢▢▢■▢▢▢ S ▢▢▢

▢▢ A ▢▢

▢▢▢▢▢ G ▢▢▢▢

▢▢▢ U ▢▢▢

▢▢ A ▢■▢▢▢

▢▢▢ R ▢▢▢▢

▢ O ▢▢▢▢

Gila monsters are the largest lizards native to the United States. While they are venomous, they tend to be sluggish and do not pose a threat to humans.

Gray foxes tend to be active from the late evening hours until dawn. They will readily climb trees, jumping from branch to branch while hunting or for protection.

Common Names
vs.
Scientific Names

A common name of an organism is a name that is based on everyday language. You have heard the common names of plants, animals, and other living things on tv, in books, and at school. Common names can also be referred to as "English" names, popular names, or farmer's name. Common names can vary from place to place. The word for a particular tree may be one thing, but that same tree has a different name in another country. Common names can even vary from region to region, even in the same country.

Scientific names, or Latin names, are given to organisms to make it possible to have uniform names for the same species. Scientific names are in Latin. You may have heard plants or animals referred to by their scientific name or at least parts of their scientific names. Latin names are also called "binomial nomenclature" which refers to a two-part naming system. The first part of the name - the generic name -names the genus to which the species belongs. The second part of the name, the specific name, identifies the species. For example, Tyrannosaurus rex is an example of a widely known scientific name.

American Black Bear

Ursus americanus

COMMON NAME

Coyote

Canis latrans

LATIN NAME = GENUS + SPECIES

Coyote = Canis latrans

Black Bear = Ursus americanus

Find the Match!
Common Names and Latin Names

Match the common name to the scientific name for each animal. The first one is done for you. Use clues on the page before and after this one to complete the matches.

Bobcat	Aquila chrysaetos
Burrobush	Canis latrans
Banana Yucca	Chordelies minor
Coyote	Taxidea taxus
Great Horned Owl	Ambrosia dumbs
Golden Eagle	Heloderma suspectum
Common Nighthawk	Bubo virginianus
American Badger	**Lynx rufus**
Gila monster	Yucca baccata

American Badger

Taxidea taxus

Nighthawk
Chordelies minor

Golden Eagle
Aquila chrysaetos

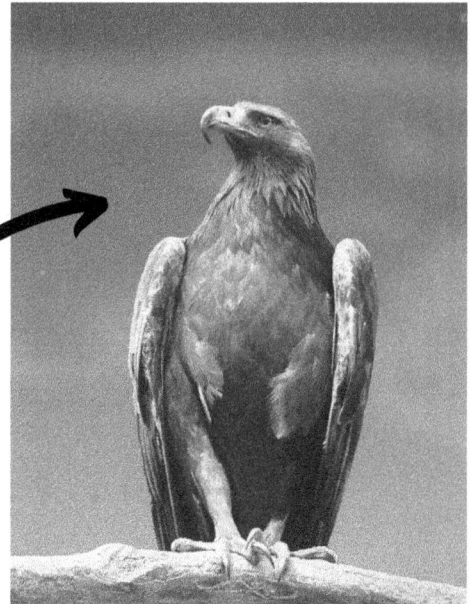

Great Horned Owl
Bubo virginianus

Some plants and animals that live at Saguaro NP

Banana Yucca
Yucca baccata

Coyote
Canis latrans

Gila Monster
Heloderma suspectum

Photobook

Draw some pictures of
things you saw in the park.

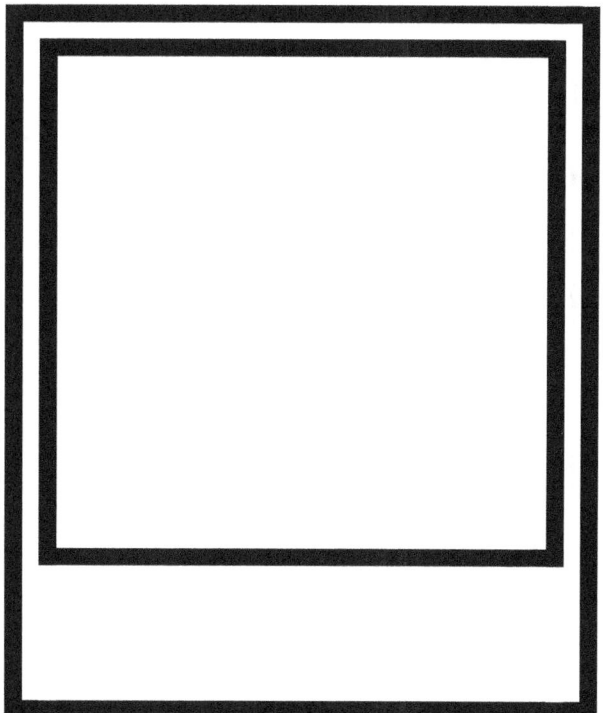

The Ten Essentials

The ten essentials is a list of things that are important to have when you go for longer hikes. If you go on a hike to the <u>backcountry</u>, it is especially important that you have everything you need in case of an emergency. If you get lost or something unforeseen happens, it is good to be prepared to survive until help finds you.

The ten essentials list was developed in the 1930s by an outdoors group called the Mountaineers. Over time and technological advancements, this list has evolved. Can you identify all the things on the current list? Circle each of the "essentials" and cross out everything that doesn't make the cut.

fire: matches, lighter, tinder and/or stove	a pint of milk	extra money	headlamp plus extra batteries	extra clothes
extra water	a dog	Polaroid camera	bug net	lightweight games, like a deck of cards
extra food	a roll of duct tape	shelter	sun protection like sunglasses, sun-protective clothes and sunscreen	knife: plus a gear repair kit
a mirror	navigation: map, compass, altimeter, GPS device, or satellite messenger	first aid kit	extra flip-flops	entertainment like video games or books

Backcountry- a remote undeveloped rural area.

20

Protecting the Park

When you visit national parks, it is important to leave the park the way you found it. Did you know that the national parks get hundreds of millions of visitors every year? We can only protect national parks for future visitors to enjoy if everyone does their part. The choices that each visitor makes when visiting the park have a big impact together.

Read each line below. Write a sentence or draw a picture to show the impacts these changes would make on the park.

What would happen if every visitor fed the wild animals?

What would happen if every visitor picked a flower?

What would happen if every visitor took home a few rocks?

What would happen if every visitor wrote or carved their name on the rocks or saguaros?

Connect the Dots #2

This animal lives in almost every state in the US, including the national park. They are nocturnal and are more active at night and sleep during the day. They are omnivorous eaters, which means they eat both plants and animals.

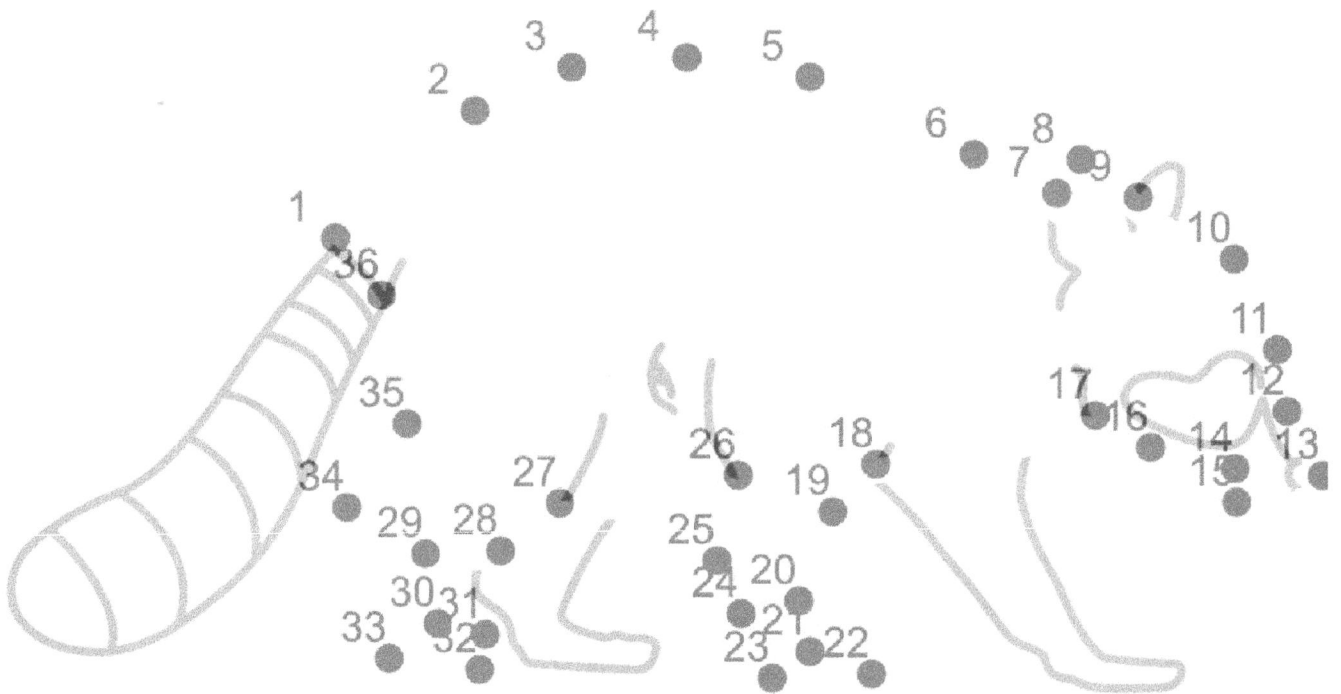

Are you an omnivore like a raccoon? An herbivore only eats plant foods. A carnivore only eats meat. An omnivore eats both. What type of eater are you? Write down some of your favorite foods to back up your answer.

_____

_____

LISTEN CAREFULLY

Visitors to Saguaro National Park may hear different noises from those they hear at home. Try this activity to experience this for yourself!

First, find a place outside where it is comfortable to sit or stand for a few minutes. You can do this by yourself or with a friend or family member. Once you have a good spot, close your eyes and listen. Be quiet for one minute and pay attention to what you are hearing. List some of the sounds you have heard in one of the two boxes below:

NATURAL SOUNDS
MADE BY ANIMALS, TREES OR PLANTS, THE WIND, ETC

HUMAN-MADE SOUNDS
MADE BY PEOPLE, MACHINES, ETC

ONCE YOU ARE BACK AT HOME, TRY REPEATING YOUR EXPERIMENT:

NATURAL SOUNDS
MADE BY ANIMALS, TREES OR PLANTS, THE WIND, ETC

HUMAN-MADE SOUNDS
MADE BY PEOPLE, MACHINES, ETC

WHERE DID YOU HEAR MORE NATURAL SOUNDS? _____

WHERE DID YOU HEAR MORE HUMAN SOUNDS? _____

Sensory Hike

Go for a sensory hike with your friends or family. Circle one activity from each sense to do along the way.

SEE

Stand in the desert. What do you think lives here based on what you see?

OR

Look for tracks, scat (poop), or other evidence of animals on the trail. Who was on the trail before you?

SMELL

Take a deep breath in three different spots on your hike. Do they smell different? Why or why not?

OR

Take notice of any strong smells you encounter. Do they smell good, bad, or somewhere in between?

HEAR

Listen to a bird sound. What do you think its call or song says?

OR

Listen to the air. Is it moving or still? What sound does it make?

TOUCH

Try to find something with a rough surface and something with a smooth surface. Why do they feel different?

OR

Sit still for a few minutes and pretend you are a baby coyote. What do you feel on the ground?

Which one was your favorite one to do? How did it make you feel?

_____

_____

_____

Saguaro Word Search

Words may be horizontal, vertical, or diagonal
and they might be backward!

1. cactus
2. water
3. Grand One
4. bats
5. Arizona
6. Manning Camp
7. fire
8. desert
9. Tucson
10. Sonoran
11. adaptation
12. species
13. monument
14. rainfall
15. Douglas
16. nighttime
17. bats
18. rattlesnakes
19. flowers
20. bees
21. tanque

```
S W S L S P E C I E S L O W D
H T A S N O S C U T E L A E J
T W A T E R O S C C L B S P R
S M N B G P R S C E R E O C A
C E O D I A S L O E R U N A I
A O Z D T U O A D T T E O S N
E M I T T H G I N N K R R C F
P L R C M U I E G W N E A A A
R M A N N I N G C A M P N D L
E C F L O W E R S I S G O E L
Q T A H C H T A N G U E N S N
S M O N U M E N T M O K I R E
I I O S H Z I D O U G L A S W
F C G O L O V O S O B R V E H
I I C A K M I N E R A E H E A
R T R A T T L E S N A K E S L
E Y D R O E L E C T R I C S E
C J A D A P T A T I O N L A M
```

25

Find the Match!
What are Baby Animals Called?

Match the animal to its baby. The first one is done for you.

Elk	eaglet
Bald Eagle	calf
Little Brown Bat	snakelets
Striped Skunk	pup
Great Horned Owl	owlet
Western Toad	kit
Mountain Lion	tadpole
Garter snake	kitten

Staying Safe in the Sun

It is important to take precautions to stay safe outdoors, especially when it is very hot outside. When someone gets overheated or dehydrated, they may feel sick or even require medical attention.

Use the cryptogram below to decode three tips on how to prevent heat-related illnesses. You may need to do some math to figure out the answers.

T _ _ _   _ _ _ _ _ _   _ _   _ _ _ _
12   5   12/2   50   30   21   50   5   2x3   36   3x4   27   21   50   6x6   12

_ _   _ _ _ _   _ _ _ _ _ .
99   10   15-3   4   50   36   7-3   5   1   50

_ _ _ _   **H** _ _ _ _ _ _ _   _ _
36   12   1x5   18   4   2x9   1   21   5   12   50   8-7   30   18

_ _ _ _ _ _ _ _ _   _ _ _ _   _ _ _ _ _ _ _ .
1   21   99   10   6   33x3   10   75   35   3x9   12   36   27   5x5   18/2   5   12   50   21

_ _ **A** _   _ _ _ _ _ _ _ _ _   _ _ _
9   50   12-7   21   36   3   10   36   15   21   5x10   50   10   5   10   12-11

_ _ _ - _ _ _ _ _ _ _ _ _
36   3   10   8   7x3   27   12   50   15   9+3   99   80   50

_ _ _ _ _ **I** **N** **G** .
15   35   27   12   2x2   99   10   75

a	b	c	d	e	f	g	h	i	j	k	l	m	n	o
5	30	15	1	50	25	75	4	99	20	6	35	49	10	27

p	q	r	s	t	u	v	w	x	y	z
8	16	21	36	12	3	80	9	40	18	7

The Perfect Picnic Spot

Fill in the blanks on this page without looking at the full story. Once you have each line filled out, use the words you've chosen to complete the story on the next page.

EMOTION _____

FOOD _____

SOMETHING SWEET _____

STORE _____

MODE OF TRANSPORTATION _____

NOUN _____

SOMETHING ALIVE _____

SAUCE _____

PLURAL VEGETABLES _____

ADJECTIVE _____

PLURAL BODY PART _____

ANIMAL _____

PLURAL FRUIT _____

PLACE _____

SOMETHING TALL _____

COLOR _____

ADJECTIVE _____

NOUN _____

A DIFFERENT ANIMAL _____

FAMILY MEMBER #1 _____

FAMILY MEMBER #2 _____

VERB THAT ENDS IN -ING _____

A DIFFERENT FOOD _____

The Perfect Picnic Spot

Use the words from the previous page to complete a silly story.

When my family suggested having our lunch at the Mica View picnic area, I was

_____. I love eating my _____ outside! I knew we had picked up a
EMOTION   FOOD

box of _____ from the _____ for after lunch, my favorite. We drove up
SOMETHING SWEET   STORE

to the area and I jumped out of the _____. "I will find the perfect spot for
MODE OF TRANSPORTATION

a picnic!" I grabbed a _____ for us to sit on, and I ran off. I passed a picnic
NOUN

table, but it was covered with _____ so we couldn't sit there. The next
SOMETHING ALIVE

picnic table looked okay, but there were smears of _____ and pieces of
SAUCE

_____ everywhere. The people that were there before must have been
PLURAL VEGETABLES

_____! I gritted my _____ together and kept walking down the path,
ADJECTIVE   PLURAL BODY PART

determined to find the perfect spot. I wanted a table with a good view of the

mountains. Why was this so hard? If we were lucky, I might even get to see

_____ eating some _____ on a cactus. They don't have those in _____
ANIMAL   PLURAL FRUIT   PLACE

where I am from. I walked down a little hill and there it was, the perfect spot!

The saguaro towered overhead and looked as tall as _____. The patch of
SOMETHING TALL

desert plants were a beautiful _____ color. The _____ flowers were
COLOR   ADJECTIVE

growing on the side of a _____. I looked across the desert and even saw a
NOUN

_____ on the edge of a rock. I looked back to see my _____ and
DIFFERENT ANIMAL   FAMILY MEMBER #1

_____ _____ a picnic basket. "I hope you brought plenty of
FAMILY MEMBER #2   VERB THAT ENDS IN ING

_____, I'm starving!"
A DIFFERENT FOOD

29

Hike to a Saguaro Forest

start here →

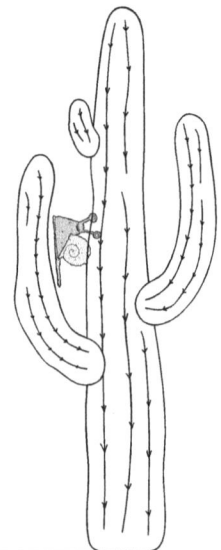

DID YOU KNOW?

Over 2 million saguaro cacti live in the national park!

All About the Saguaro

The saguaro cactus is the largest in the world! It is native only to the Sonoran desert. While the average saguaro can grow up to 40 feet tall, they grow slowly. In the national park, studies show that a saguaro grows about 1 to 1.5 inches in the first eight years of its life.

1. spines
2. flowers
3. arms
4. cactus
5. desert
6. columnar
7. bats
8. bees
9. birds
10. fruit
11. ribs
12. seeds
13. nests
14. tall
15. dry

```
L D E S S U L P Y R D E O W T
H A D D E S E R T W E R W I H
T V D N U I T T A W A L U O A
S E U T S P S U C Y U R B M L
C N C A E Q Y A L E F R S K L
M A D L Y R R K C T L E I O E
C O L U M N A R R H O R L A B
A R B E M K I R D I W S V N E
L B H O G I L O M O E D E P E
L I I R S M O Y K S R G R T S
I R A U A S E N I P S B N C N
S D N S K A O I S A S K T R E
T S O S B H I N Z R I B S O C
E Y G T A L L E I N D S V E O
R W E L T O R A D O A E H E M
T T E L S R E E N L A E E N T
U A E E S T S E N O A D V E B
C J D W I K E E R C Y S I O N
```

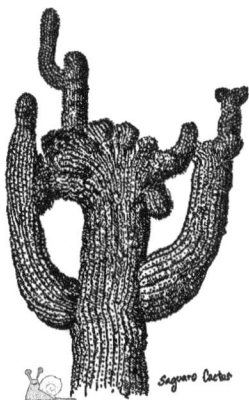

Saguaro Cactus

Leave No Trace Quiz

Leave No Trace is a concept that helps people make decisions during outdoor recreation that protects the environment. There are seven principles that guide us when we spend time outdoors, whether you are in a national park or not. Are you an expert in Leave No Trace? Take this quiz and find out!

1. How can you plan ahead and prepare to ensure you have the best experience you can in the national park?
   a. Make sure you stop by the ranger station for a map and to ask about current conditions.
   b. Just wing it! You will know the best trail when you see it.
   c. Stick to your plan, even if conditions change. You traveled a long way to get here, and you should stick to your plan.
2. What is an example of traveling on a durable surface?
   a. Walking only on the designated path.
   b. Walking on the grass that borders the trail if the trail is very muddy.
   c. Taking a shortcut if you can find one since it means you will be walking less.
3. Why should you dispose of waste properly?
   a. You don't need to. Park rangers love to pick up the trash you leave behind.
   b. You actually should leave your leftovers behind, because animals will eat them. It is important to make sure they aren't hungry.
   c. So that other peoples' experiences of the park are not impacted by you leaving your waste behind.
4. How can you best follow the concept "leave what you find"?
   a. Take only a small rock or leaf to remember your trip.
   b. Take pictures, but leave any physical items where they are.
   c. Leave everything you find, unless it may be rare like an arrowhead, then it is okay to take.
5. What is not a good example of minimizing campfire impacts?
   a. Only having a campfire in a pre-existing campfire ring.
   b. Checking in with current conditions when you consider making a campfire.
   c. Building a new campfire ring in a location that has a better view.
6. What is a poor example of respecting wildlife?
   a. Building squirrel houses out of rocks so the squirrels have a place to live.
   b. Stay far away from wildlife and give them plenty of space.
   c. Reminding your grown-ups to not drive too fast in animal habitats while visiting the park.
7. How can you show consideration of other visitors?
   a. Play music on your speaker so other people at the campground can enjoy it.
   b. Wear headphones on the trail if you choose to listen to music.
   c. Make sure to yell "Hello!" to every animal you see at top volume.

Park Poetry

America's parks inspire art of all kinds. Painters, sculptors, photographers, writers, and artists of all mediums have taken inspiration from natural beauty. They have turned their inspiration into great works.

Use this space to write your own poem about the park. Think about what you have experienced or seen. Use descriptive language to create an acrostic poem. This type of poem has the first letter of each line spell out another word. Create an acrostic that spells out the word "Desert."

D _____

E _____

S _____

E _____

R _____

T _____

Desert landscape

Everywhere you look

Saguaros strech tall

Enchanting views

Restorative

Take me back

Driving forever

Enjoying family

Singing silly songs

Excited

Ready to see

Towering saguaros

Making a Difference

It is important to protect the valuable resources of the world, not just beautiful places like national parks.

How many of these things do you do at home? If you answered "no" to more than 10 items, talk to the grownups in your life to see if there are any household habits you might be able to change. Conserving our collective resources helps us all.

Yes	No	Do you...
☐	☐	turn off the water when you are brushing your teeth?
☐	☐	use LED light bulbs when possible?
☐	☐	use a reusable water bottle instead of disposable ones?
☐	☐	ride your bike or take the bus instead of riding in the car?
☐	☐	have a rain barrel under your roof gutters to collect rain water?
☐	☐	take quick showers?
☐	☐	avoid putting more food on your plate than you will eat?
☐	☐	take reusable lunch containers?
☐	☐	grow a garden?
☐	☐	buy items with less packaging?
☐	☐	recycle paper?
☐	☐	recycle plastic?
☐	☐	have a compost pile at home so you can make your own soil?
☐	☐	pick up trash when you see it on the trail?
☐	☐	plan a "staycation" and fly only when you have to?

_____   _____

\# of   \# of
Yes   No

Add up your score! Are there any "no"s that you want to turn into a yes?

Can you think of any other ways to protect our natural resources?

Hungry, Hungry Gila Monster

start here

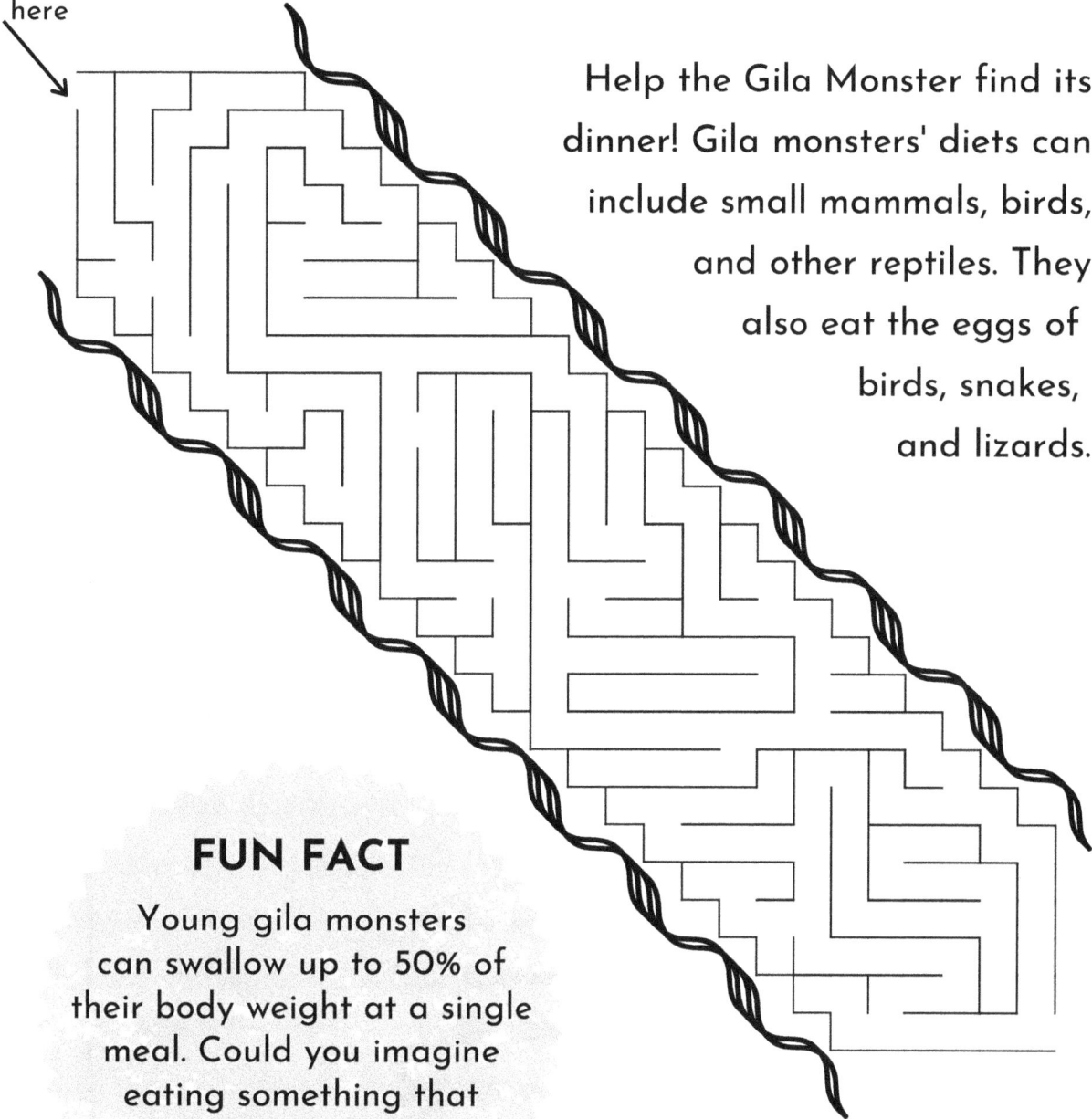

Help the Gila Monster find its dinner! Gila monsters' diets can include small mammals, birds, and other reptiles. They also eat the eggs of birds, snakes, and lizards.

FUN FACT

Young gila monsters can swallow up to 50% of their body weight at a single meal. Could you imagine eating something that weighs half as much as you at one sitting?

Stacking Rocks

Have you ever seen stacks of rocks while hiking in national parks? Do you know what they are or what they mean? These rock piles are called cairns and often mark hiking routes in parks. Every park has a different way to maintain trails and cairns. However, they all have the same rule: If you come across a cairn, do not disturb it.

Color the cairn and the rules to remember.

1. Do not tamper with cairns.

If a cairn is tampered with or an unauthorized one is built, then future visitors may become disoriented or even lost.

2. Do not build unauthorized cairns.

Moving rocks disturbs the soil and makes the area more prone to erosion. Disturbing rocks can disturb fragile plants.

3. Do not add to existing cairns.

Authorized cairns are carefully designed. Adding to them can actually cause them to collapse.

Decoding Using American Sign Language

American Sign Language, also called ASL for short, is a language that many Deaf people or people who are hard of hearing use to communicate. People use ASL to communicate with their hands. Did you know people from all over the country and world travel to national parks? You may hear people speaking other languages. You might also see people using ASL. Use the American Manual Alphabet chart to decode some national parks facts.

This was the first national park to be established:

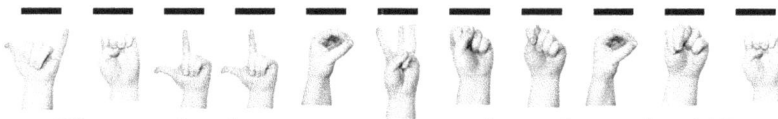

_ _ _ _ _ _ _ _ _ _

This is the biggest national park in the US:

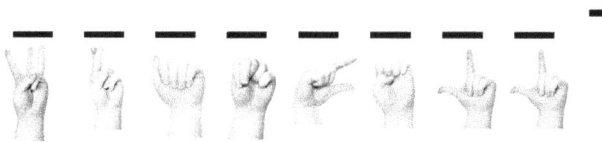

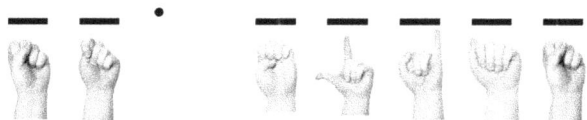

_ _ _ _ _ _ _ -

_ _ . _ _ _ _

This is the most visited national park:

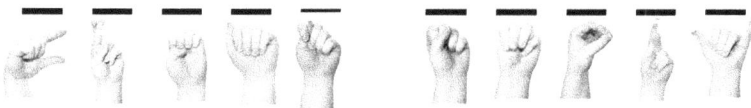

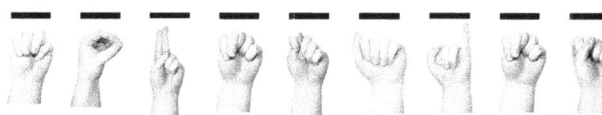

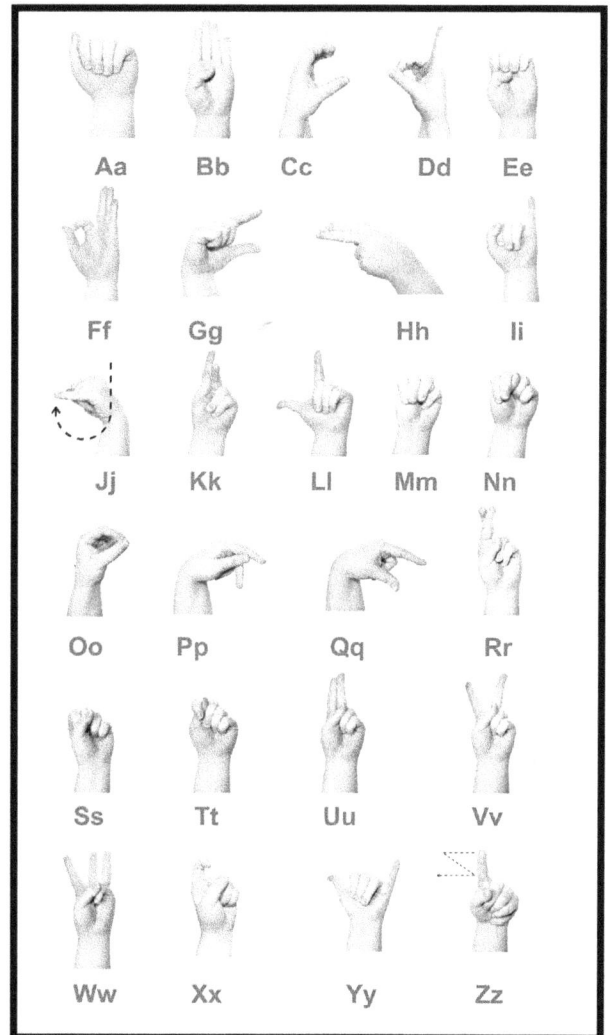

_ _ _ _ _ _ _ _

_ _ _ _ _ _ _ _ _

Aa	Bb	Cc	Dd	Ee
Ff	Gg		Hh	Ii
Jj	Kk	Ll	Mm	Nn
Oo	Pp		Qq	Rr
Ss	Tt		Uu	Vv
Ww	Xx		Yy	Zz

Hint: Pay close attention to the position of the thumb!

Try it! Using the chart, try to make the letters of the alphabet with your hand. What is the hardest letter to make? Can you spell out your name? Show a friend or family member and have them watch you spell out the name of the national park you are in.

Go Horseback Riding on the Signal Hill Trail

Help find the horse's lost shoe!

start
here

DID YOU KNOW?

Horseback riding is a popular activity in Saguaro National Park. There are many trails that you can take horses for day or overnight trips.

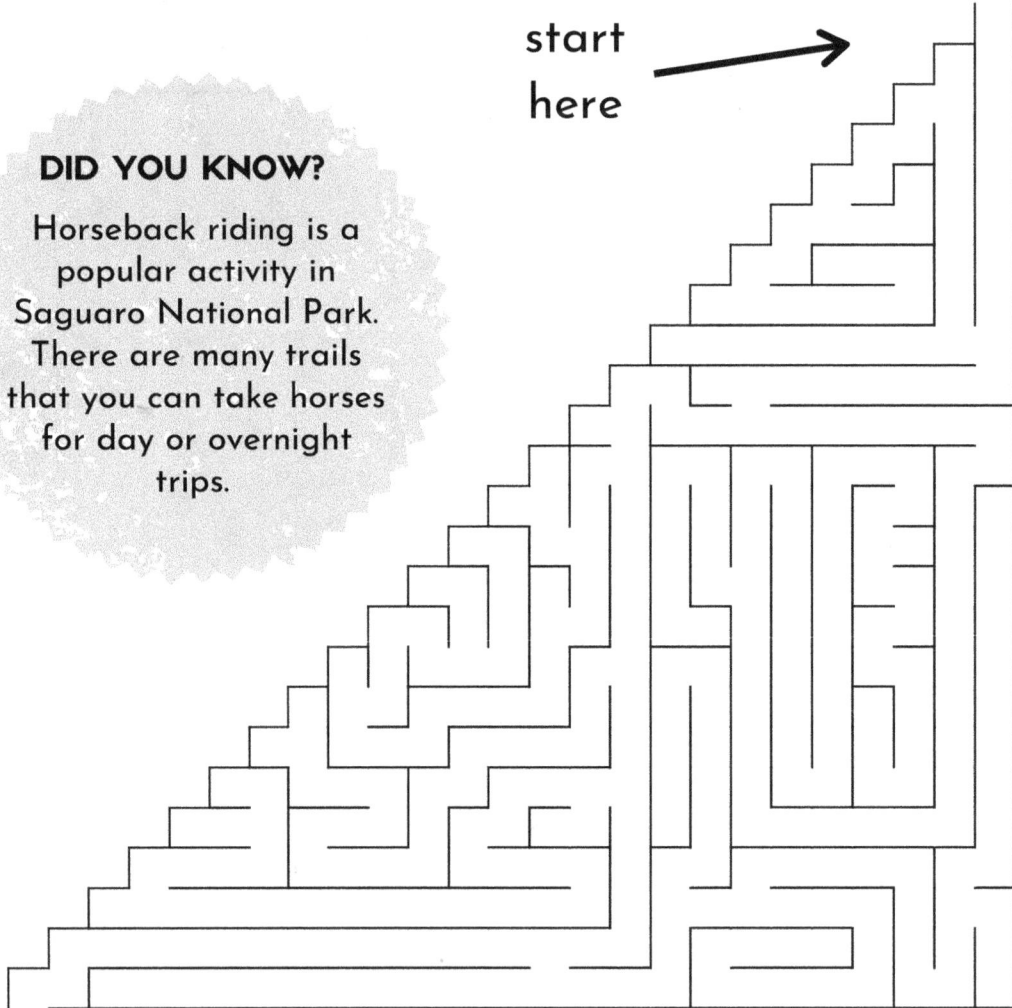

Butterflies of the Sonoran Desert

Dozens of species of butterflies and moths live in Saguaro National Park. Their wingspan size varies, as do the patterns on their wings. Design your own butterfly below. Make sure the wings are symmetrical, meaning both sides match.

A Hike at King Canyon

Fill in the blanks on this page without looking at the full story. Once you have each line filled out, use the words you've chosen to complete the story on the next page.

ADJECTIVE _____

SOMETHING TO EAT _____

SOMETHING TO DRINK _____

NOUN _____

ARTICLE OF CLOTHING _____

BODY PART _____

VERB _____

ANIMAL _____

SAME TYPE OF FOOD _____

ADJECTIVE _____

SAME ANIMAL _____

VERB THAT ENDS IN "ED" _____

NUMBER _____

A DIFFERENT NUMBER _____

SOMETHING THAT FLIES _____

LIGHT SOURCE _____

PLURAL NOUN _____

FAMILY MEMBER _____

YOUR NICKNAME _____

A Hike at King Canyon

Use the words from the previous page to complete a silly story.

I went for a hike at King Canyon today. In my favorite _ _ _ _ _ _ backpack, I
ADJECTIVE

made sure to pack a map so I wouldn't get lost. I also threw in an extra

_ _ _ _ _ _ _ _ _ _ just in case I got hungry and a bottle of _ _ _ _ _ _ _ _ _ _. I put
SOMETHING TO EAT   SOMETHING TO DRINK

on my _ _ _ _ _ _ _ _ _ spray, and a tied a _ _ _ _ _ _ _ _ _ _ _ around my
NOUN   ARTICLE OF CLOTHING

_ _ _ _ _ _ _ _ _, in case it gets chilly. I started to _ _ _ _ _ _ down the path. As
BODY PART   VERB

soon as I turned the corner, I came face to face with a(n) _ _ _ _ _ _ _ _. I think
ANIMAL

it was as startled as I was! What should I do? I had to think fast! Should I

give it some of my _ _ _ _ _ _ _ _ _ _? No. I had to remember what the
SAME TYPE OF FOOD

_ _ _ _ _ _ _ ranger told me. "If you see one, back away slowly and try not to
ADJECTIVE

scare it." Soon enough, the _ _ _ _ _ _ _ _ _ _ _ _ _ _ _ _ _ _ away. The coast
SAME ANIMAL   VERB THAT ENDS IN ED

was clear. _ _ _ _ _ _ hours later, I finally got to the lookout. I felt like I could
NUMBER

see for a _ _ _ _ _ _ miles. I took a picture of a _ _ _ _ _ _ _ _ so I could always
A DIFFERENT NUMBER   NOUN

remember this moment. As I was putting my camera away, a _ _ _ _ _ _ _ _ _
SOMETHING THAT FLIES

flew by, reminding me that it was almost nighttime. I turned on my

_ _ _ _ _ _ _ _ _ and headed back. I could hear the _ _ _ _ _ _ _ _ _ _ singing their
LIGHT SOURCE   PLURAL INSECT

evening song. Just as I was getting tired, I saw my _ _ _ _ _ _ _ _ _ and our tent.
FAMILY MEMBER

"Welcome back _ _ _ _ _ _ _! How was your hike?"
NICKNAME

41

Design a Badge

Imagine you've been hired to create a badge that will be for sale in the Rincon Mountain Visitor Center. Your badge will be a souvenir for visitors to remember their trip to the park.

Consider adding a plant or animal that lives here, or include a famous place in the park or activity that you can do while visiting.

Let's Go Camping Word Search

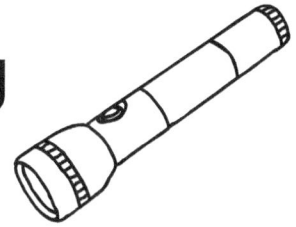

Words may be horizontal, vertical, or diagonal and they might be backward!

1. tent
2. camp stove
3. sleeping bag
4. bug spray
5. sunscreen
6. map
7. flashlight
8. pillow
9. lantern
10. ice
11. snacks
12. smores
13. water
14. first aid kit
15. chair
16. cards
17. books
18. games
19. trail
20. hat

```
D P P I L L O W D B T E A C I
E O A D P R E A A M B R C A N
P W C A M P S T O V E I H X G
R A H S G E L E B E E D A P S
E L B U G S P R A Y N G I E A
S I A H G C I C N N M E R C N
C W N L A F I R S K O O B F K
M T A E M I L E L H M R W L J
T A P R E A O R E S L B A A B
S M P A S R R T E N T L U S C
C E A I I R C G P E I U J H A
S S N A C K S S I M O K I L R
I J R S F O I S N J R A Q I D
C Y E T L E V E G U O R V G S
E W T A K C A B B S S O H H M
X J N F I R S T A I D K I T T
U A A E S S E N G E T P V A B
C J L I A R T D N A M A H A S
```

All in the Day of a Park Ranger

Park Rangers are hardworking individuals dedicated to protecting our parks, monuments, museums, and more. They take care of the natural and cultural resources for future generations. Rangers also help protect the visitors of the park. Their responsibilities are broad and they work both with the public and behind the scenes.

What have you seen park rangers do? Use your knowledge of the duties of park rangers to fill out a typical daily schedule, one activity for each hour. Feel free to make up your own, but some examples of activities are provided on the right. Read carefully, not all of the example activities are befitting a ranger!

Time	Activity
6 am	Lead a sunrise hike
7 am	
8 am	
9 am	
10 am	
11 am	
12 pm	Enjoy a lunch break outside
1 pm	
2 pm	
3 pm	
4 pm	Teach visitors about the geology of the desert
5 pm	
6 pm	
7 pm	
8 pm	
9 pm	

- feed the golden eagles
- build trails for visitors to enjoy
- throw rocks off the side of the mountain
- rescue lost hikers
- study animal behavior
- record air quality data
- answer questions at the visitor center
- pick wildflowers
- pick up litter
- share marshmallows with squirrels
- repair handrails
- lead a class on a field trip
- catch frogs and make them race
- lead people on educational hikes
- write articles for the park website
- protect rivers and streams from pollution
- remove non-native plants from the park
- study how climate change is affecting the park
- give a talk about mountain lions
- lead a program for campers on javelina

If you were a park ranger, which of the above tasks would you enjoy most?

_____

44 _____

Draw Yourself as a Park Ranger

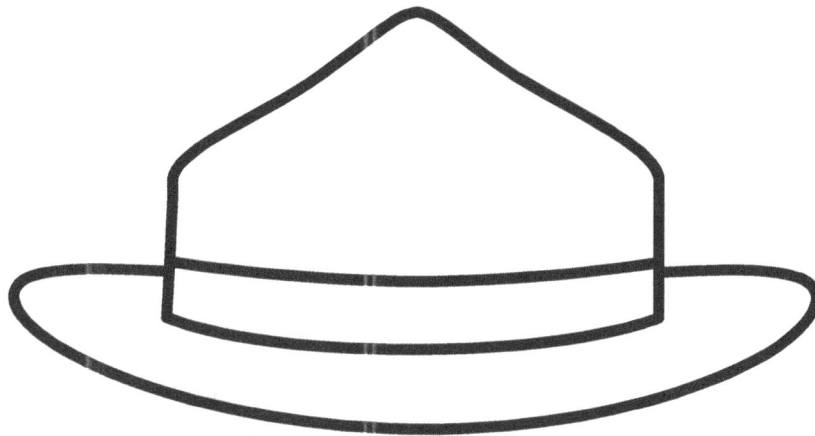

RANGER

Rattlesnakes of Saguaro

1. IRTEG

The park is home to several species of rattlesnakes. Each species has a different color pattern. Unscramble the species names that live in the park.

2. L CATIK BLADE

3. RIE RAPI

4. OPIH

Word Bank

Prairie
Timber
Hopi
Tiger
Mojave
Speckled
Dusky
Great Basin
Blacktailed

5. JO VAME

1.- _____
2.- _____
3.- _____
4.- _____
5.- _____

Amphibians

Five species of toad and three species of frogs live in Saguaro Park. Frogs and toads both spend the beginning of their lives the same way, as tadpoles. Tadpoles hatch from eggs in water, usually in springs or pools of water.

Both frogs and toads are amphibians. Salamanders are amphibians too. Color the amphibians below.

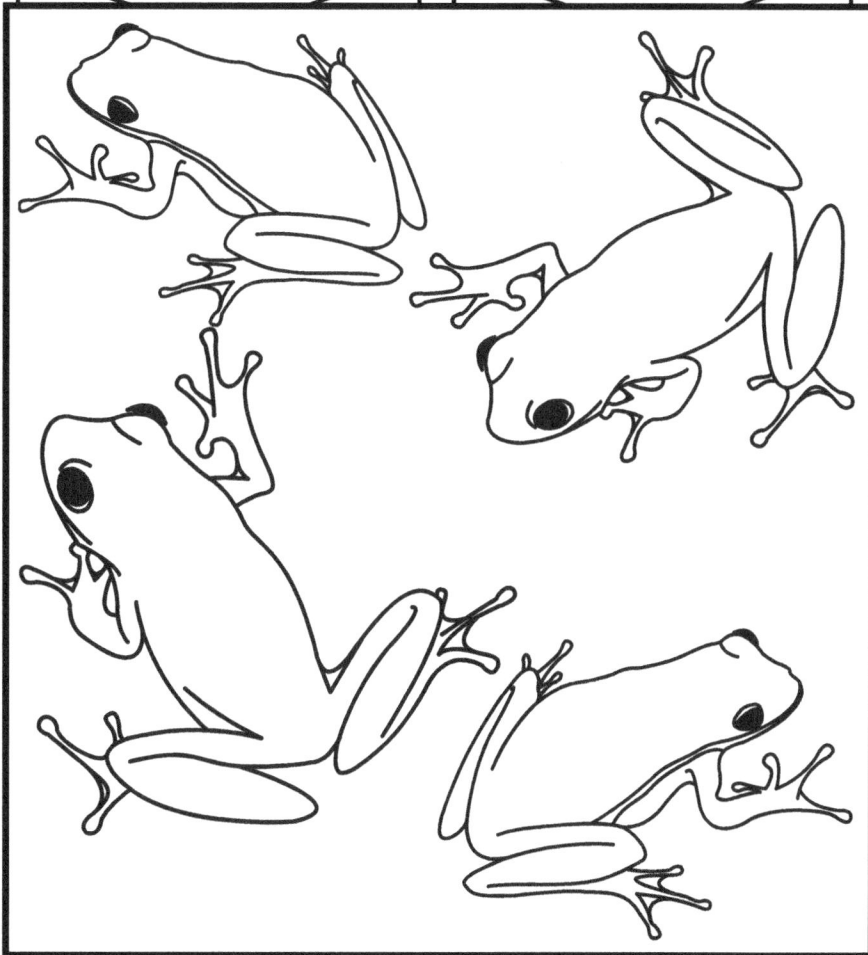

The Dazzling Desert

People come from all over the world to experience the wonders of the desert at Saguaro National Park. If you are able to see the desert for yourself, make some observations. Draw or describe them in the boxes below, using lots of detail.

Something colorful	A desert rock	Something that moves
An insect	Something cool you saw	A tiny plant
Something with a smell	A leaf	Something shiny

Being Respectful

Rangers need your help! Some people toss their trash where they shouldn't, create graffiti, or take artifacts when they visit Saguaro National Park. Create a poster to help show other visitors how to be respectful in the space below.

63 National Parks

How many other national parks have you been to? Which one do you want to visit next? Note that some of these parks fall on the border of more than one state, you may check it off more than once!

Alaska
- ☐ Denali National Park
- ☐ Gates of the Arctic National Park
- ☐ Glacier Bay National Park
- ☐ Katmai National Park
- ☐ Kenai Fjords National Park
- ☐ Kobuk Valley National Park
- ☐ Lake Clark National Park
- ☐ Wrangell-St. Elias National Park

American Samoa
- ☐ National Park of American Samoa

Arizona
- ☐ Grand Canyon National Park
- ☐ Petrified Forest National Park
- ☐ Saguaro National Park

Arkansas
- ☐ Hot Springs National Park

California
- ☐ Channel Islands National Park
- ☐ Death Valley National Park
- ☐ Joshua Tree National Park
- ☐ Kings Canyon National Park
- ☐ Lassen Volcanic National Park
- ☐ Pinnacles National Park
- ☐ Redwood National Park
- ☐ Sequoia National Park
- ☐ Yosemite National Park

Colorado
- ☐ Black Canyon of the Gunnison National Park
- ☐ Great Sand Dunes National Park
- ☐ Mesa Verde National Park
- ☐ Rocky Mountain National Park

Florida
- ☐ Biscayne National Park
- ☐ Dry Tortugas National Park
- ☐ Everglades National Park

Hawaii
- ☐ Haleakalā National Park
- ☐ Hawai'i Volcanoes National Park

Idaho
- ☐ Yellowstone National Park

Kentucky
- ☐ Mammoth Cave National Park

Indiana
- ☐ Indiana Dunes National Park

Maine
- ☐ Acadia National Park

Michigan
- ☐ Isle Royale National Park

Minnesota
- ☐ Voyageurs National Park

Missouri
- ☐ Gateway Arch National Park

Montana
- ☐ Glacier National Park
- ☐ Yellowstone National Park

Nevada
- ☐ Death Valley National Park
- ☐ Great Basin National Park

New Mexico
- ☐ Carlsbad Caverns National Park
- ☐ White Sands National Park

North Dakota
- ☐ Theodore Roosevelt National Park

North Carolina
- ☐ Great Smoky Mountains National Park

Ohio
- ☐ Cuyahoga Valley National Park

Oregon
- ☐ Crater Lake National Park

South Carolina
- ☐ Congaree National Park

South Dakota
- ☐ Badlands National Park
- ☐ Wind Cave National Park

Tennessee
- ☐ Great Smoky Mountains National Park

Texas
- ☐ Big Bend National Park
- ☐ Guadalupe Mountains National Park

Utah
- ☐ Arches National Park
- ☐ Bryce Canyon National Park
- ☐ Canyonlands National Park
- ☐ Capitol Reef National Park
- ☐ Zion National Park

Virgin Islands
- ☐ Virgin Islands National Park

Virginia
- ☐ Shenandoah National Park

Washington
- ☐ Mount Rainier National Park
- ☐ North Cascades National Park
- ☐ Olympic National Park

West Virginia
- ☐ New River Gorge National Park

Wyoming
- ☐ Grand Teton National Park
- ☐ Yellowstone National Park

Other National Parks

Besides Saguaro National Park, there are 62 other diverse and beautiful national parks across the United States. Try your hand at this crossword. If you need help, look at the previous page for some hints.

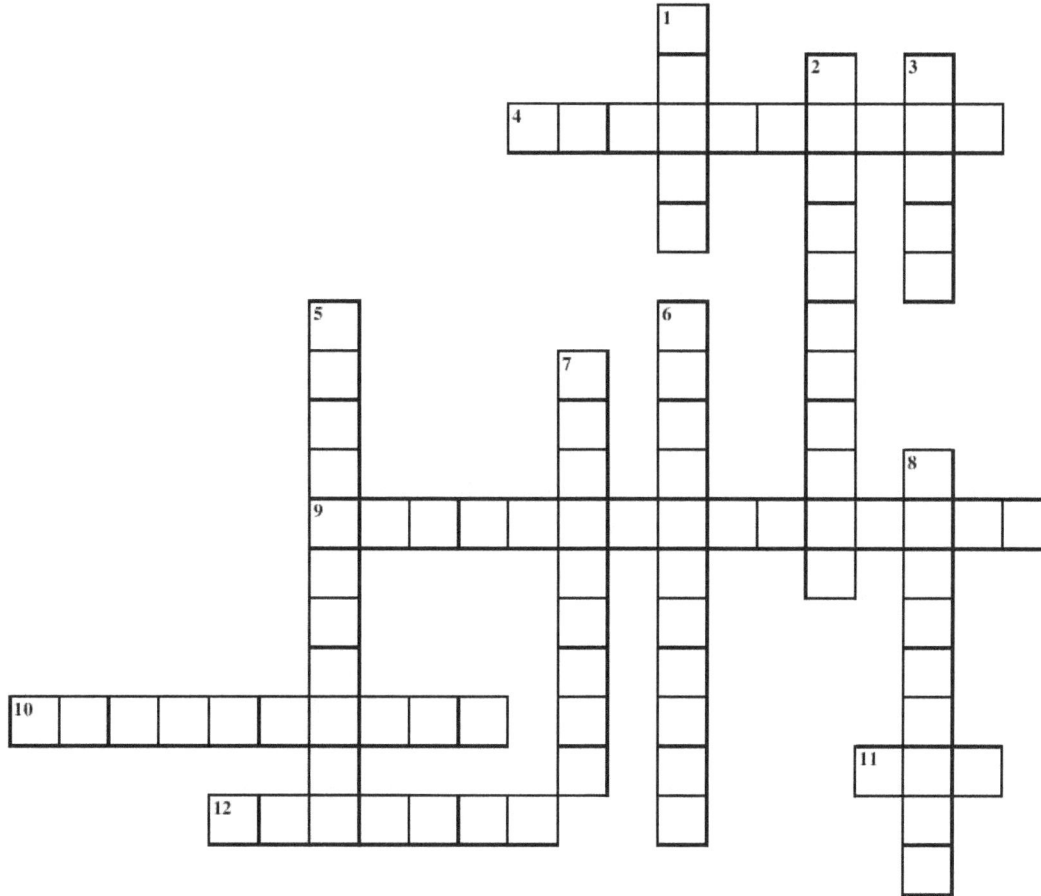

Down

1. State where Acadia National Park is located
2. This national park has the Spanish word for turtle in it.
3. Number of national parks in Alaska
5. This national park has some of the hottest temperatures in the world.
6. This national park is the only one in Idaho.
7. This toothsome creature can be famously found in Everglades National Park.
8. Only president with a national park named for them

Across

4. This state has the most national parks.
9. This park has some of the newest land in the US, caused by volcanic eruptions.
10. This park has the deepest lake in the United States.
11. This color shows up in the name of a national park in California.
12. This national park deserves a gold medal.

Which National Park Will You Go to Next?
Word Search

1. Zion
2. Big Bend
3. Glacier
4. Olympic
5. Sequoia
6. Bryce
7. Mesa Verde
8. Biscayne
9. Wind Cave
10. Great Basin
11. Katmai
12. Yellowstone
13. Voyageurs
14. Arches
15. Badlands
16. Denali
17. Glacier Bay
18. Hot Springs

```
F M M E S A V E R D E B N E Y
E A B I G B E N D E S A S E M
Y L I C A L O Y N E E D L T G
D M G A S S A U C N R L U E R
C E L I I T S C R E O A A K E
S N A W Y E E O I W T N A C A
G I C H A A Q C S E M D N S T
N O I Z P R U T I M R S N E B
I W E L M P O N B W E B K H A
R J R F D N I F L I H B U C S
P A B E E S A N E S O P W R I
S J A E N Y A C S I B A U A N
T C Y I A D O H H Y M E A L R
O T A T L M L E S E G R W R J
H S T O I K A T M A I R O P B
I C H U R C O L Y M P I C O U
O Y G T S D E O S B R Y C E T
W I N D C A V E I N R O H E M
```

Field Notes

Spend some time to reflect on your trip to Saguaro National Park. Your field notes will help you remember the things you experienced. Use the space below to write about your day.

While I was at Saguaro National Park...

I saw:

_____

_____

_____

_____

I heard:

_____

_____

_____

_____

I felt:

_____

_____

Draw a picture of your favorite thing in the park.

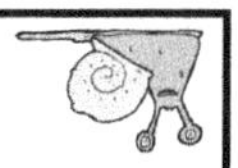

I wondered:

ANSWER KEY

National Park Emblem Answers

1. This represents all plants. **Sequoia Tree**

2. This represents all animals. **Bison**

3. This symbol represents the landscapes. **Mountains**

4. This represents the waters protected by the park service. **Water**

5. This represents the historical and archeological values. **Arrowhead**

Jumbles Answers

1. READING

2. HIKING

3. BIRDING

4. CAMPING

5. PICNICKING

6. SIGHTSEEING

7. STAR GAZING

Go Birdwatching at Bridal Wreath Falls

start here

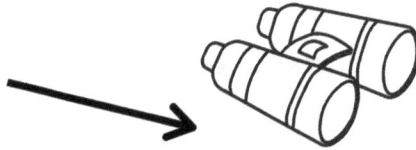

DID YOU KNOW?
Saguaro NP is home to several birds of prey, including eagles, hawks, and owls. Birds of prey are birds that hunt other animals for food.

Answers: Who lives here?

Here are seven plants and animals that live in the park.
Use the word bank to fill in the clues below.

WORD BANK: HUMMINGBIRD, COATI, SCORPION, GILA MONSTER
BOBCAT, GRAY FOX, SAGUARO

GILA █ MON S TER

CO A TI

HUMMIN G BIRD

SAG U ARO

GR A Y █ FOX

SCO R PION

B O BCAT

Find the Match!
Common Names and Latin Names

Match the common name to the scientific name for each animal. The first one is done for you. Use clues on the page before and after this one to complete the matches.

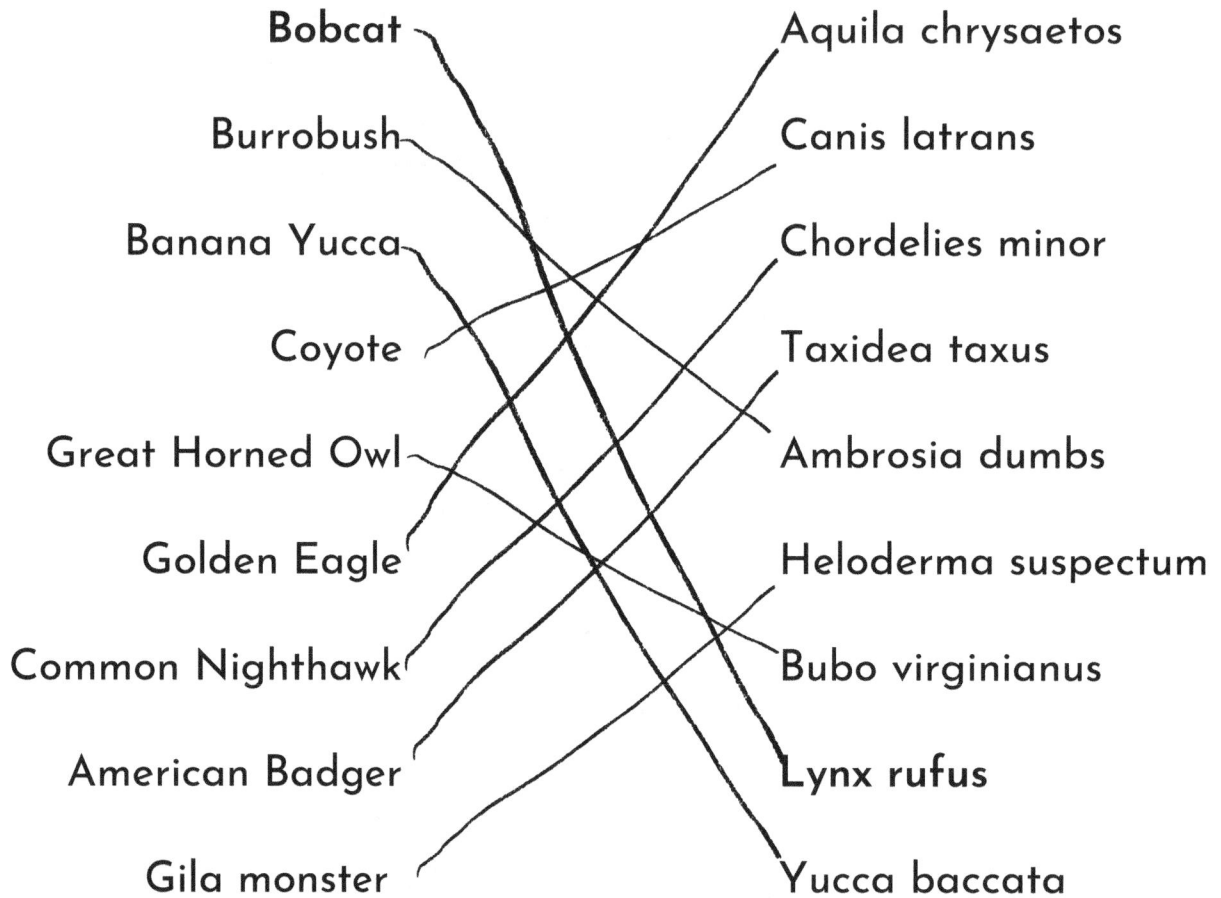

Bobcat — Aquila chrysaetos

Burrobush — Canis latrans

Banana Yucca — Chordelies minor

Coyote — Taxidea taxus

Great Horned Owl — Ambrosia dumbs

Golden Eagle — Heloderma suspectum

Common Nighthawk — Bubo virginianus

American Badger — Lynx rufus

Gila monster — Yucca baccata

American Badger

Taxidea taxus

Answers: The Ten Essentials

The ten essentials is a list of things that are important to have when you go for longer hikes. If you go on a hike to the <u>backcountry</u>, it is especially important that you have everything you need in case of an emergency. If you get lost or something unforeseen happens, it is good to be prepared to survive until help finds you.

The ten essentials list was developed in the 1930s by an outdoors group called the Mountaineers. Over time and technological advancements, this list has evolved. Can you identify all the things on the current list? Circle each of the "essentials" and cross out everything that doesn't make the cut.

(fire: matches, lighter, tinder and/or stove)	~~a pint of milk~~	~~extra money~~	(headlamp plus extra batteries)	(extra clothes)
(extra water)	~~a dog~~	~~Polaroid camera~~	~~bug net~~	~~lightweight games like a deck of cards~~
(extra food)	~~a roll of duct tape~~	(shelter)	(sun protection like sunglasses, sun-protective clothes and sunscreen)	(knife: plus a gear repair kit)
~~a mirror~~	(navigation: map, compass, altimeter, GPS device, or satellite messenger)	(first aid kit)	~~extra flip flops~~	~~entertainment like video games or books~~

Backcountry- a remote undeveloped rural area.

Saguaro Word Search

Words may be horizontal, vertical, or diagonal
and they might be backward!

1. cactus
2. water
3. Grand One
4. bats
5. Arizona
6. Manning Camp
7. fire
8. desert
9. Tucson
10. Sonoran
11. adaptation
12. species
13. monument
14. rainfall
15. Douglas
16. nighttime
17. bats
18. rattlesnakes
19. flowers
20. bees
21. tanque

```
S W S L S P E C I E S L O W D
H T A S N O S C U T E L A E J
T W A T E R O S C C L B S P R
S M N B G P R S C E R E O C A
C E O D I A S L O E R U N A I
A O Z D T U O A D T T E O S N
E M I T T H G I N N K R R C F
P L R C M U I E G W N E A A A
R M A N N I N G C A M P N D L
E C F L O W E R S I S G O E L
Q T A H C H T A N G U E N S N
S M O N U M E N T M O K I R E
I I O S H Z I D O U G L A S W
F C G O L O V O S O B R V E H
I I C A K M I N E R A E H E A
R T R A T T L E S N A K E S L
E Y D R O E L E C T R I C S E
C J A D A P T A T I O N L A M
```

Answers: Find the Match!
What are Baby Animals Called?

Match the animal to its baby. The first one is done for you.

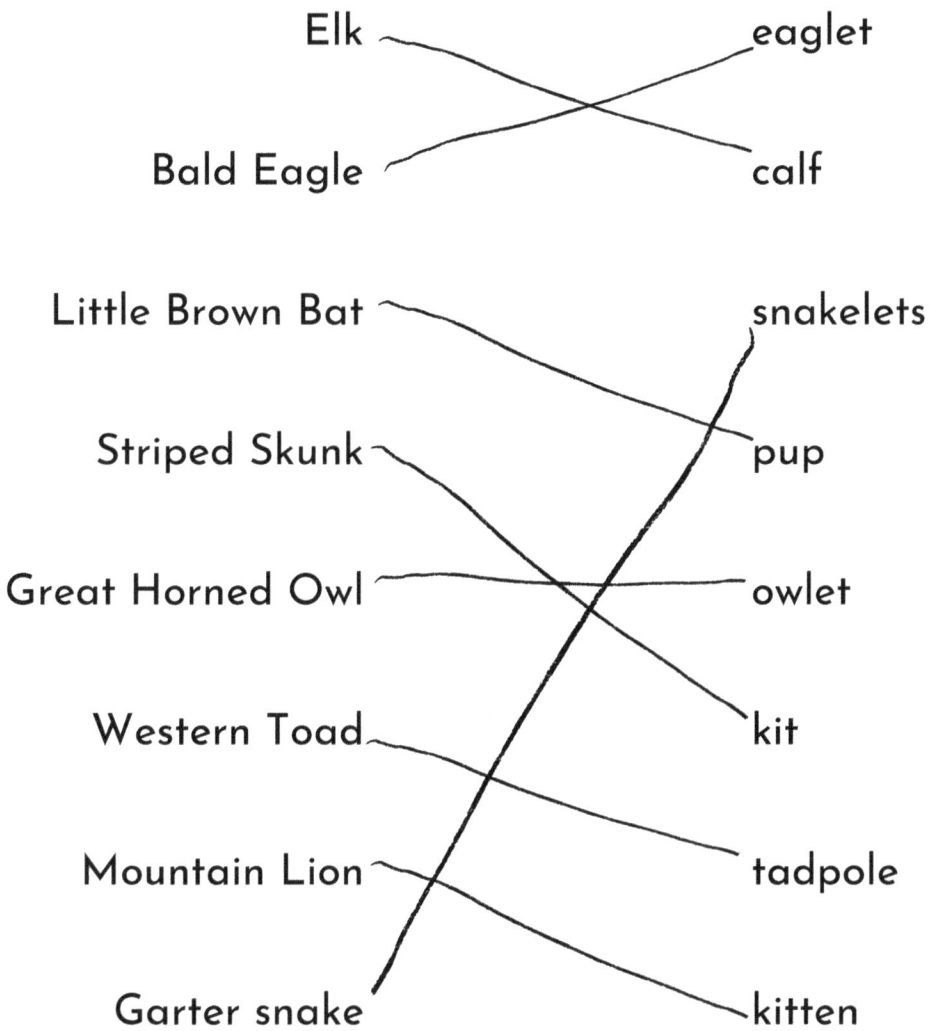

Elk — eaglet

Bald Eagle — calf

Little Brown Bat — snakelets

Striped Skunk — pup

Great Horned Owl — owlet

Western Toad — kit

Mountain Lion — tadpole

Garter snake — kitten

Solution: Hike to a Saguaro Forest

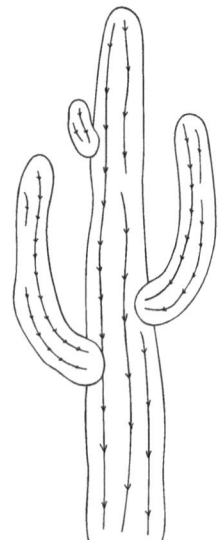

All About the Saguaro

1. spines
2. flowers
3. arms
4. cactus
5. desert
6. columnar
7. bats
8. bees
9. birds
10. fruit
11. ribs
12. seeds
13. nests
14. tall
15. dry

```
L D E S S U L P Y R D E O W T
H A D D E S E R T W E R W I H
T V D N U I T T A W A L U O A
S E U T S P S U C Y U R B M L
C N C A E Q Y A L E F R S K L
M A D L Y R R K C T L E I O E
C O L U M N A R R H O R L A B
A R B E M K I R D I W S V N E
L B H O G I L O M O E D E P E
L I I R S M O Y K S R G R T S
I R A U A S E N I P S B N C N
S D N S K A O I S A S K T R E
T S O S B H I N Z R I B S O C
E Y G T A L L E I N D S V E O
R W E L T O R A D O A E H E M
T T E L S R E E N L A E E N T
U A E E S T S E N O A D V E B
C J D W I K E E R C Y S I O N
```

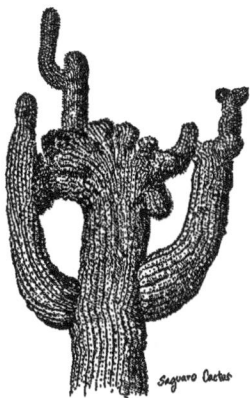

Saguaro Cactus

63

Answers: Leave No Trace Quiz

Leave No Trace is a concept that helps people make decisions during outdoor recreation that protects the environment. There are seven principles that guide us when we spend time outdoors, whether you are in a national park or not. Are you an expert in Leave No Trace? Take this quiz and find out!

1. How can you plan ahead and prepare to ensure you have the best experience you can in the National Park?

    A. Make sure you stop by the ranger station for a map and to ask about current conditions.

2. What is an example of traveling on a durable surface?

    A. Walking only on the designated path.

3. Why should you dispose of waste properly?

    C. So that other peoples' experiences of the park are not impacted by you leaving your waste behind.

4. How can you best follow the concept "leave what you find"?

    B. Take pictures but leave any physical items where they are.

5. What is not a good example of minimizing campfire impacts?

    C. Building a new campfire ring in a location that has a better view.

6. What is a poor example of respecting wildlife?

    A. Building squirrel houses out of rocks from the river so the squirrels have a place to live.

7. How can you show consideration of other visitors?

    B. Wear headphones on the trail if you choose to listen to music.

Hungry, Hungry Gila Monster

start here

Help the Gila Monster find its dinner! Gila monsters' diets can include small mammals, birds, and other reptiles. They also eat the eggs of birds, snakes, and lizards.

FUN FACT

Young gila monsters can swallow up to 50% of their body weight at a single meal. Could you imagine eating something that weighs half as much as you at one sitting?

Decoding Using American Sign Language

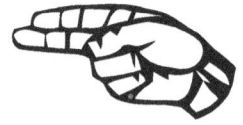

American Sign Language, also called ASL for short, is a language that many Deaf people or people who are hard of hearing use to communicate. People use ASL to communicate with their hands. Did you know people from all over the country and world travel to national parks? You may hear people speaking other languages. You might also see people using ASL. Use the American Manual Alphabet chart to decode some national parks facts.

This was the first national park to be established:

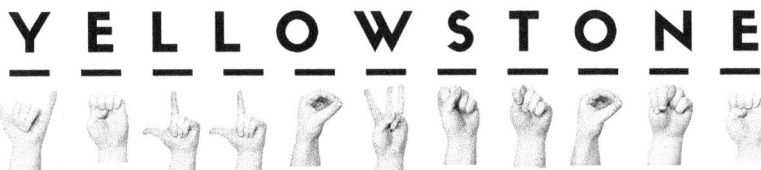

Y E L L O W S T O N E

This is the biggest national park in the US:

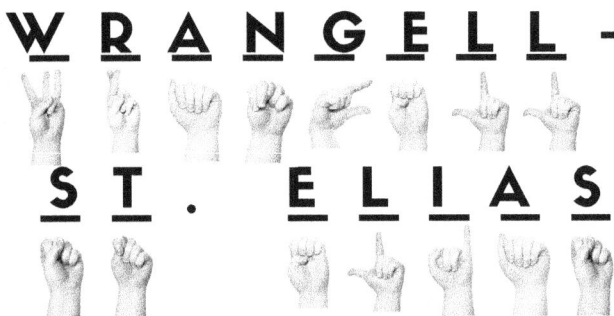

W R A N G E L L -

S T . E L I A S

This is the most visited national park:

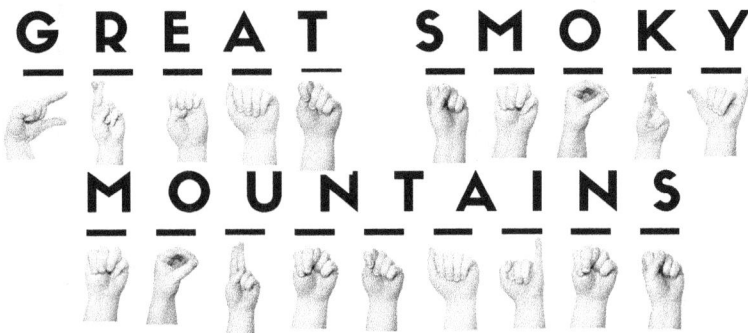

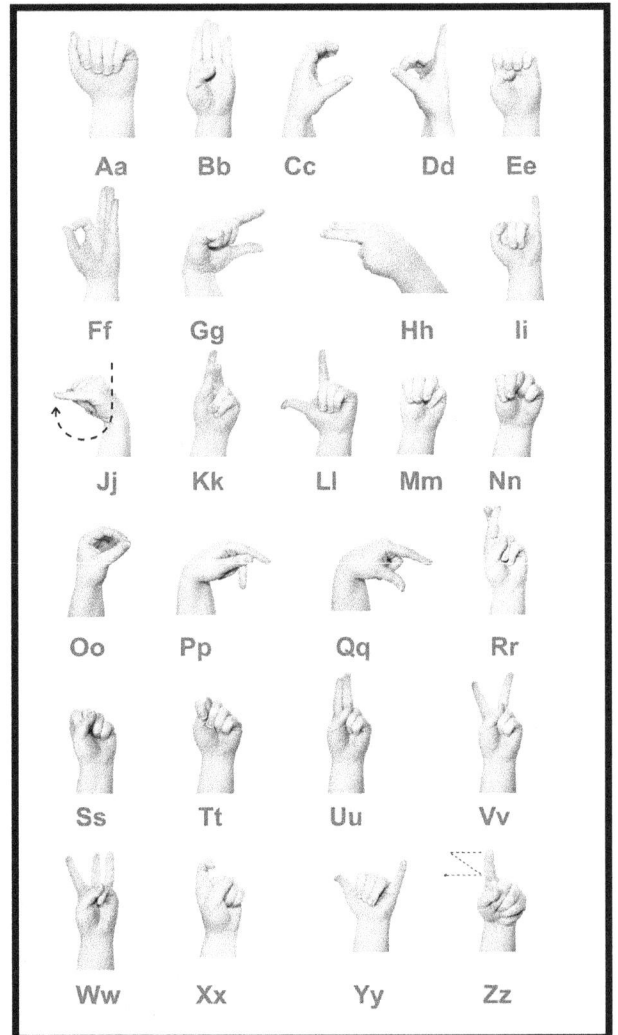

G R E A T   S M O K Y

M O U N T A I N S

Aa	Bb	Cc	Dd	Ee
Ff	Gg		Hh	Ii
Jj	Kk	Ll	Mm	Nn
Oo	Pp		Qq	Rr
Ss	Tt	Uu		Vv
Ww	Xx	Yy	Zz	

Hint: Pay close attention to the position of the thumb!

Try it! Using the chart, try to make the letters of the alphabet with your hand. What is the hardest letter to make? Can you spell out your name? Show a friend or family member and have them watch you spell out the name of the national park you are in.

Go Horseback Riding on the Signal Hill Trail

Help find the horse's lost shoe!

start here →

DID YOU KNOW?

Horseback riding is a popular activity in Saguaro National Park. There are many trails that you can take horses for day or overnight trips.

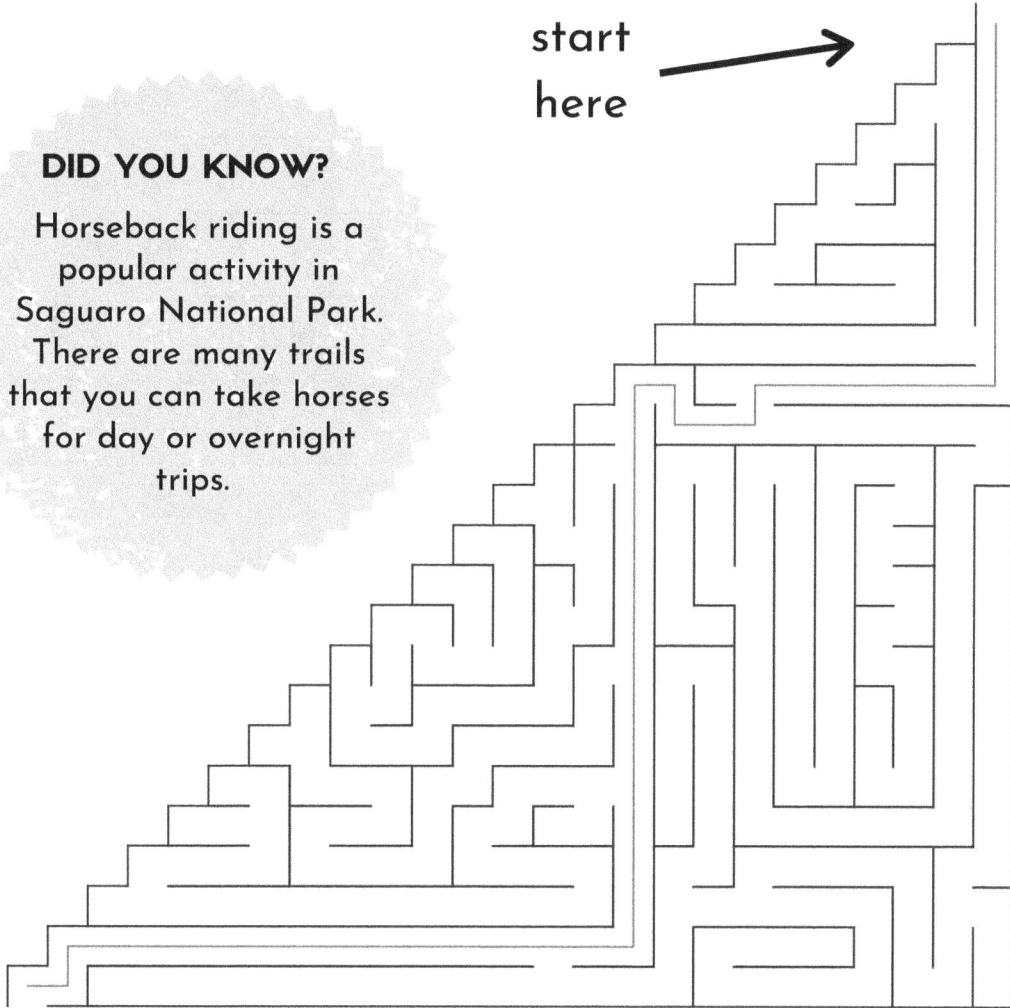

Let's Go Camping
Word Search

1. tent
2. camp stove
3. sleeping bag
4. bug spray
5. sunscreen
6. map
7. flashlight
8. pillow
9. lantern
10. ice
11. snacks
12. smores
13. water
14. first aid kit
15. chair
16. cards
17. books
18. games
19. trail
20. hat

```
D P P I L L O W D B T E A C I
E O A D P R E A A M B R C A N
P W C A M P S T O V E I H X G
R A H S G E L E B E E D A P S
E L B U G S P R A Y N G I E A
S I A H G C I C N N M E R C N
C W N L A F I R S K O O B F K
M T A E M I L E L H M R W L J
T A P R E A O R E S L B A A B
S M P A S R R T E N T L U S C
C E A I I R C G P E I U J H A
S S N A C K S S I M O K I L R
I J R S F O I S N J R A Q I D
C Y E T L E V E G U O R V G S
E W T A K C A B B S S O H H M
X J N F I R S T A I D K I T T
U A A E S S E N G E T P V A B
C J L I A R T D N A M A H A S
```

68

Solution:
Rattlesnakes of Saguaro

1.

IRTEG

The park is home to several species of rattlesnakes. Each species has a different color pattern. Unscramble the species names that live in the park.

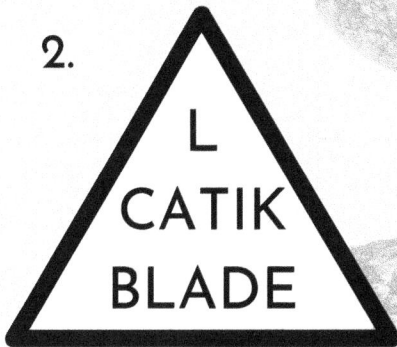

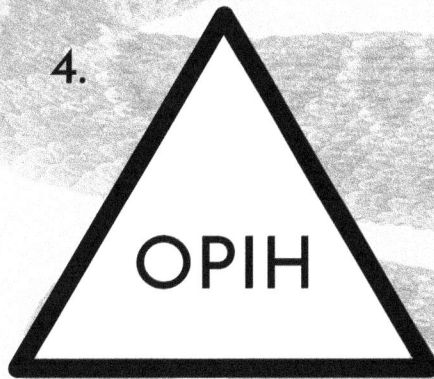

2.

L CATIK BLADE

3.

RIE RAPI

Word Bank

Prairie
Timber
Hopi
Tiger
Mojave
Speckled
Dusky
Great Basin
Blacktailed

4.

OPIH

5.

JO VAME

1. TIGER
2. BLACKTAILED
3. PRAIRIE
4. HOPI
5. MOJAVE

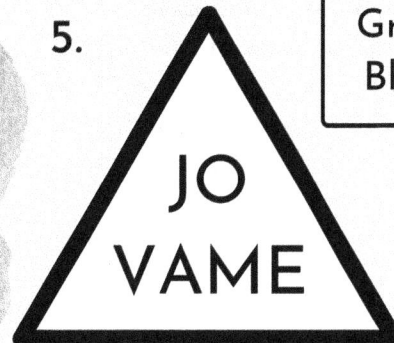

Answers: Other National Parks

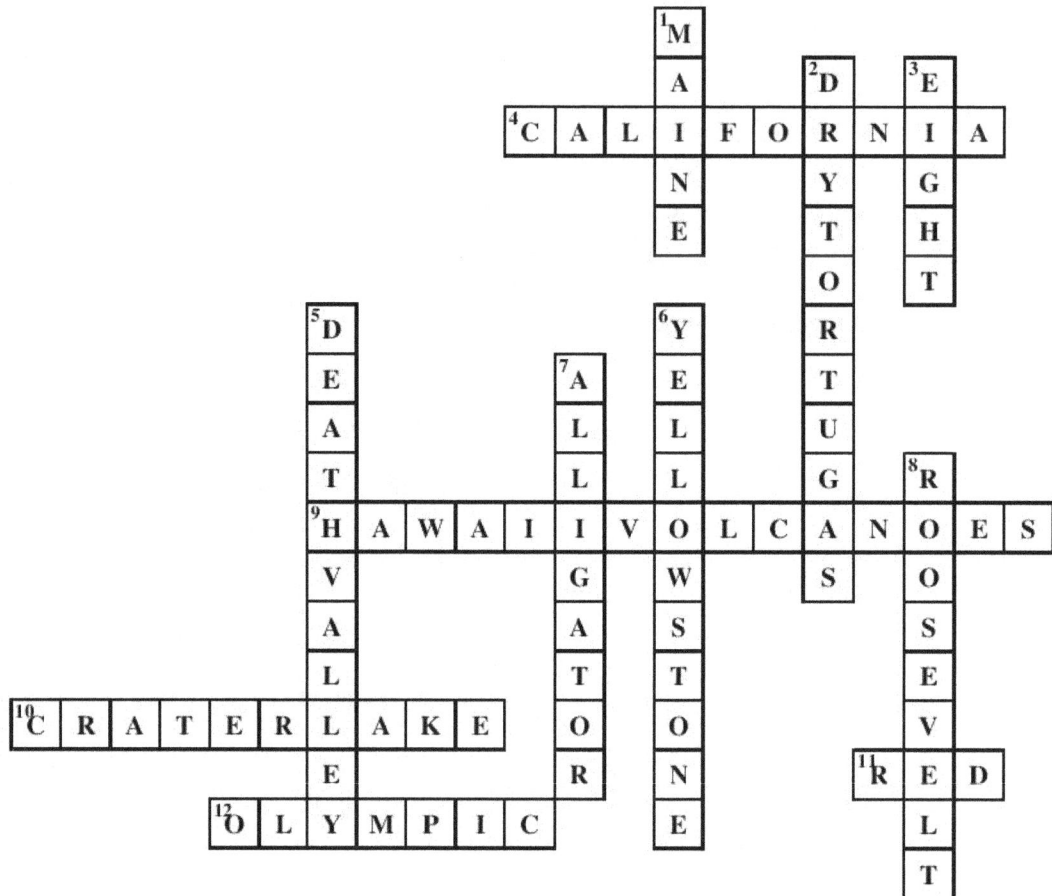

Crossword grid (answers):

- 1 Down: MAINE
- 2 Down: DRYTORTUGAS
- 3 Down: EIGHT
- 4 Across: CALIFORNIA
- 5 Down: DEATHVALLEY
- 6 Down: YELLOWSTONE
- 7 Down: ALLIGATOR
- 8 Down: ROOSEVELT
- 9 Across: HAWAIIVOLCANOES
- 10 Across: CRATERLAKE
- 11 Across: RED
- 12 Across: OLYMPIC

Down

1. State where Acadia National Park is located
2. This National Park has the Spanish word for turtle in it
3. Number of National Parks in Alaska
5. This National Park has some of the hottest temperatures in the world
6. This National Park is the only one in Idaho
7. This toothsome creature can be famously found in Everglades National Park
8. Only president with a national park named for them

Across

4. This state has the most National Parks
9. This park has some of the newest land in the US, caused by a volcanic eruption
10. This park has the deepest lake in the United States
11. This color shows up in the name of a National Park in California
12. This National Park deserves a gold medal

Answers: Where National Park Will You Go Next?

1. Zion
2. Big Bend
3. Glacier
4. Olympic
5. Sequoia
6. Bryce
7. Mesa Verde
8. Biscayne
9. Wind Cave
10. Great Basin
11. Katmai
12. Yellowstone
13. Voyageurs
14. Arches
15. Badlands
16. Denali
17. Glacier Bay
18. Hot Springs

F M M E S A V E R D E B N E Y
E A B I G B E N D E S A S E M
Y L I C A L O Y N E E D L T G
D M G A S A U C N R L U E R E
C E L I I T S C R E O A A K A
S N A W Y E E O I W T N A C A
G I C H A A Q C S E M D N S T
N O I Z P R U T I M R S N E B
I W E L M P O N B W E B K H A
R J R F D N I F L I H B U C S
P A B E E S A N E S O P W R I
S J A E N Y A C S I B A U A N
T C Y I A D O H H Y M E A L R
O T A T L M L E S E G R W R J
H S T O I K A T M A I R O P B
I C H U R C O L Y M P I C O U
O Y G T S D E O S B R Y C E T
W I N D C A V E I N R O H E M